Poems on the Paintings of Matisse

Nick Monks

Bluebell Publishing

Title Page

Poems on the Paintings of Matisse- Nick Monks

Copyright © 2020 by Nick Monks

All rights reserved. No part of this publication may be reproduced, distributed, or transmitted in any form or by any means, including photocopying, recording, or other electronic or mechanical methods, without the prior written permission of the publisher, except in the case of brief quotations embodied in critical reviews and certain other non- commercial uses permitted by copyright law.

Published June 2020

Printed by Lulu
www.lulu.com

ISBN: 978-1-9163546-7-8

For Amanda, Karl, Saskia

CONTENTS

Preface   Page 5

The Joy of Life   Page 9
Bathers with a Turtle   10
11AD   11
Music   12
The Beasts of the Sea   13
A Nude Standing Before an Open Door   14
Woman on a High Stool   15
Bathers by a River   16
Antibes   17
Annelies, White Tulips and Anemones   18
Aht Amont Cliffs at Etretat   19
Blue Nude 11   20
Woman with a Hat   21
The Snail   22
Notre Dame, 1902   23
The Dance, 1910   24
The Conversation   25
The Dessert: Harmony in Red   26
Woman Reading   27
Woman in a Purple Coat   28
The Open Window   29

PREFACE

Henri Emile Benoit Matisse- 31st December 1869 to 3rd November 1954, was a French artist known for his use of colour and original draftsmanship. Was one of the Fauves (Wild Beasts) from 1900 to 1905

With Pablo Picasso defined the change to the modern. The two met in 1906. Relocated to Nice, southern France from Paris, in 1917. He was diagnosed with abdominal cancer in 1941 and surgery left him chair and bedbound. With assistants he made paper cut out collages. His colours in paintings are intense. He makes use of multiple patterns in many of his paintings.

He grew up in Bohain- En- Vermandois in Picardy, Northern France. His father was a grain merchant. He studied art at the Academie Julian in Paris. Married to Amelie Parayre who divorced him in 1939, as he was probably having an affair with Lydia Delectorskaya. During his Fauve phase a critic said "a pot of paint has been thrown into the face of the public" Gertrude Stein bought his paintings. And Apollinaire was complementary. After 1930 his paintings were more- bold and simplified. Stayed in Vichy France during the German occupation.

His *Plum Blossoms* 1948 was purchased by the Museum of Modern Art in 2005 for an estimated $25m. He died in 1954.

Credits: Much of the above information is credited to Wikipedia entry.

Poems on the Paintings of Matisse

The Joy of Life

Arcadian scene with pastel colours overarched by trees foliage. Women and a few men in repose or movement. Welcoming the playground city of trees. An orchestra meets an architect and plans Avalon. The figures simple and stylized. Sumptuous and brazen.

There is no need for a house. Or a bank. Or shops. Or offices. Home is this overarching beauty. Cradled in paint juice. A beach. A wood. A galaxy of satiated wishes. Arcadia.

Bathers with a Turtle

Three young attractive women. Toy with a tiny turtle. On a sickly green grass. There is maybe a river. There is the deep troubled disconcerting sky. The women are nude. And attractive, like treacle and cinnamon. The song is a tune from Pluto.

Us vulnerable penitents. Empty before a vast sky. As the blond/ red- haired/ and black- haired girl. Toy intently with a tiny turtle. The viewer with attraction and temptation. The girl's bodies and grass and river and sky. Blotched and bruised. But still an enchanted Avalon.

11 AD

Grass. Blue deep infinity sky. Five crouched figures. All red and red. Listen to pipes and a violin. The figures are non- sexualized. Non dance. They crouch like rabbits before a bounding weasel. Transfixed by a music right, millennium old. They listen to Edith Piaf songs. Beneath the endless blue skies, deep monochrome blue

The musicians learnt their violin and pipes at childhood. The first song has been heard 1001 times. And is as familiar as a blue door. In house you've never seen. But dream of every night all your life. The house by an Avalon lake. Entranced by Sibelius 5th symphony they listen. Bright red like roses or the sun or red fish. Red crouched figures in searing simplicity listening to the songs of Edith Piaf and Vera Lynn. In 8 AD.

Music

Patterned grey ferns on a wall. A nude in red stockings. A music score by a red apple. As a woman in blue dress plays a small guitar. Both women are twin sirens. Red tiles and red wall.

Play music for me like as I was eight. Remember the Breton forests. The alighting from at the Atlantic. We have come to dance. Jewelled room. Outside silver pulsing stars.

Refugees we left the fields with rotting barley. We escaped Paris. To the red room. with two beautiful women. One nude like granite ocean rocks. Sequester the evening with music in the verdant room.

The Beasts of the Sea

Luscious symbols. Stylized shapes. In a fantasia of colour. Yellows. Mauves. Light greens. Two long rectangles like partitions of a door. Or mirrors side by side which reflect each other. Strange black beasts. Decorations for a black soul. Decorations for a lilac soul.

Speaking with effervescent charm. A rendered world by a pauper a tramp. Like Aztec or American Indians or Aborigines. A sound of the Atlantic on Brittany cliffs. The secret secluded sand cove found by two. A lullaby. The new cave drawings. Two mirrors which reflect each other. But are totally different.

A Nude Standing Before an Open Door

Woman with red/brown hair. Appealing lines of her body. Attractive enticing. Viewed sideways. With a red door? Perhaps closing the yellow curtains. A wall of tiles in light purple. Her body undone and beautiful.

A window. Her supine grace. And thousands of oceans and bridges over azure rivers. She gazes at us. But not quite. With elan and in a strange and exotic room.

Woman on a High Stool

Portrait of Germaine Raynal, wife of poet and critic Maurice Raynal. Early 1914. The woman in shapes. Cubes, circles, spheres. Sits on a high stool. Red table- top and grey room. A picture of a black and white bird on the wall.

Her face is dignified. And contains quizzical acidy. Her skirt is blue like a river or canal. Her top grey black with yellow sashes. She is an enchanted and brazen being. Trepid princess of a non-purpose grey room.

Bathers by a River

Planes of colour. Stylized grass. Four figures dissected/ deconstructed/ rendered. Without the need for the painter to add their detailed heads. Blue plain. White plain. Black plain. Grass plain. One figure crouched.

Non like coronavirus lockdown appear to talk to each other. Be in communication. The communication between the artist and his four subjects is intense. Three figures are I think women. One is a crouched man.

Each figure is indomitable. And has a terrible dignity. The stylization of the human condition.

Antibes

A woman who is pretty. Long copiously flowing skirt. Hair done up in black. Older in years. Creative thick brush strokes. In a yellow chair. Splodges of blue surround her.

She considers. Is at ease. Relishes the cool Antibes evening air. After a good day. She with two interlocked hands meditates without being aware on the turning dark blue sky. Perhaps on a house veranda. Her skirt a bloom of fine linen. Dark red top.

And the evening air is cold now. In this sequestered evening. This waiting full of hope.

Annelies: White Tulips and Anemone

A woman dishevelled but beautiful. Sitting in a chair. With an open illustrated book. White tulips in a vase on the desk. Another vase of flowers. A snap- shot of jewelled existence. Patterned background. A table of grey with white lines.

The woman exists frozen in trepid exactitude. Born of creativity. Gazing out at the viewer. Like a redolent princess of the adorned office? Disquieting. A rendered impenetrable demeanour. With her mind on appointments and work policies. Bravely gazing in divine poise.

Aht Amont Cliffs at Etretat

Beautiful shore. With cliffs and day trippers on the beach. Ships/boats on the sand sea slippage. A multi blue sea. Bedecked with beauty. Cliffs of white adorn the scape in the distance.

Expressionist largesse. Such brazen beauty. Such an idyll. Would you not like to be here. In an exquisitely crafted dream. The black figurines of beach visitors receding further down the beach. A trepid sky over the sea, the sand, the cliffs.

Blue Nude 11

Collage of shapes. Blue like sky/ocean/bluebells. Bluebells on a wood slope in spring. Her blue eyes. The figurine a woman. As pure as milled flour by a stream, the mill wheel and sails. Extolling womanhood and man- kind. Tempestuous. Arms one over- head. One draped by her side. Legs curled. Simplicity and beauty. Daring. A cool portrait in delicious shade.

Woman with a Hat

Woman bedecked by colour. A patterned rainbow. Looking unhappily from under a voluptuous hat. A still life. Patches of multi colours in the background. Her person swamped by finery and rich shades. She is as impenetrable as a river of blue and yellow. Unfortunately she has been consumed by array. Yet her red hair. Her face make up. Bequeath a quintessential essence.

The Snail

Mme Lydia Delectorskaya helped with the collage made in the hotel Regina in Nice. The paper is in multi colours. Depicting a snail or cities. Orange border and a simplification that is refreshing. Blazen country scene. A vast metropolis of border colour, planes, space.

Made while he was bed and chair ridden. A vivid dream. Ocean storm. Vast radiant Paris parks. A sunset. And artist capturing the essential. A journey inwards.

Notre Dame, 1902

Blue scape of the Seine river. Passers-by on the quay sides. A bridge over the Seine. The twin squares of Notre Dame against the sky. As they have done for centuries. Red houses. The shadow of a bridge on water.

Viewed from a window. The view rectangle. Bathed in blue. The history past pageantry. People passing to go to work or home. In Charlemagne's reign. In the deep blue light of artistic Paris.

The Dance, 1910

Dance me to the end of love. Though cities harbour mass poverty. With all gone except green grass and deep blue sky. In a circle five dance. Enraptured. Engrossed their supine bodies. Circling hands clasped. Naked. A blue- print of humanity.

A revelry. A deep mystery. An eternal transformation. A song without accompanying instruments. A blue sky. Green grass. Circling five figures to bare basic naked. Together in the human anthem of silence and awe.

The Conversation

A man against deep radiant blue. Stands in banal pyjamas and talks to a beautiful wife in black dress with green sash. Outside is the first ever garden. With black iron work window balcony.

She looks at him from the blue chair merged with the blue room. They conversation every day. A building of everyday conversations. In a world they don't understand. But within the radiant blue room. Chat in the cool shade. Illuminated. The chosen. Between them words of visual silence.

The Dessert: Harmony in Red

A table merges into the wall. A window of green. Chair with gold/yellow.

Bedazzling plentitude. Still life's trace across the arid hurtingly barren room.

The fingers of a gracious god ordain a rich dark red. As the lady in an enchanted room.

Toys with hidden. So we are within in plentitude.

Woman Reading

Patterns shimmer and repeat themselves. While a woman also with patterned skirt

Reads at a circular table with flowers in a vase. Four different sorts of patterns. Blue/red/yellow/brown, grey. Jar against each other. The woman looks around and is engrossed in the book

She has a white flower in her jet black hair. The scene is an ordered embellishment of a ordinary room with a beautiful woman reading

Woman in a Purple Coat

Woman reclining on a chair. Around her are patterns of wall and floor. A still life on a table

The woman has a striped purple coat. Her face is questioning but at ease. She carries erasure and verdant promises and terrible love. She is a seamstress of lake side houses. In an intricate adorned patterned room

The Open Window

Drear day in. You open the lounge window. Light cascades like silk. Boats in the harbour. The call of the sea. The call of the harbour town

Multi flower pots. The ivy a suburban mountaineer. Pastels, bespoke shadow and shade. The air welcome and in newness. Sail away from Le Conquet, Brittany harbour. Into the terrible fresh kiss of the sea. The boats. The cool draft. The loaf of bread cut on the kitchen table. Patterns of routines and living.

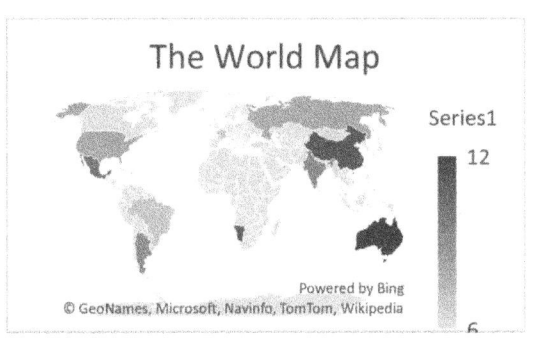

www.ingramcontent.com/pod-product-compliance
Lightning Source LLC
Chambersburg PA
CBHW031509040426
42444CB00007B/1268